HERTFORDSHIRE PRIVIES

by

RICHARD WHITMORE

D1514378

COUNTRYSIDE BOOKS

NEWBURY • BERKSHIRE

First published 1998
© Richard Whitmore 1998

COUNTRYSIDE BOOKS
3 Catherine Road
Newbury, Berkshire

ISBN 1 85306 520 X

Produced through MRM Associates Ltd., Reading
Printed by J. W. Arrowsmith Ltd., Bristol

Contents

FOREWORD

A Hertfordshire author on loos
On paper held very strong views.
From a privy he'd come
With print on his bum
Just for once, all behind with the news.

To begin with, I wasn't at all sure this idea would work. It seemed to me that a disused shit-house is the last thing anyone would keep as a social memento. I also had doubts that the folk who had used them would want to 'go public' with their recollections of intimate moments spent communing with nature all those years ago. And if they did, surely, there would not be enough reminiscences to fill a book.

However, my publishers know far more about these things than I do and they explained that their *Privies* series had proved very popular in other parts of the country. So I took their advice and sent a letter to Hertfordshire's local papers, inviting personal contributions for my latest literary project. Not surprisingly the subject matter made me the butt of a series of embarrassingly corny headlines, ranging from 'Here Is The Loos' to 'Richard Becomes A Privy Counsellor'. But it was all worthwhile because the postbag of replies was impressive. Not only that, I found myself being stopped in the street by people who had a privy tale to tell. Total strangers of both sexes revealing quite personal details of their old 'bucket-and-chuck-it' days, keen to advise me on such topics as smells, nightsoil men and which newspapers were best for wiping the bottom.

Yet, while privy *yarns* were plentiful, would there be enough privies still standing to provide the all-important illustrations for this record of our county's sanitary history? After all, most had been built of wood so, as Hertfordshire's population quadrupled and more land vanished under new developments, there was a grave danger that none had survived. In that respect, my search came just in time – because surviving thunderboxes are now few and far between.

At the same time their very rarity made each discovery an event of some excitement. The best were found in the north and east of the county, where villages and hamlets have suffered less interference from developers. Here, one can still see some good examples of the different models that stood in our backyards and cottage gardens during the first half of the century. The traditional one-holers, with box seat and soil bucket. A few two-holers as well – and in quite good condition! In the appropriately-named parish of Thundridge I found one two-seater which had a smaller hole for children, set lower than the adult one. Did the little ones really sit there beside Mother or Father to learn the art of defecation? Nowadays, when most of us prefer complete privacy on such occasions, one wonders what on earth went on in the matey three-seater model still in existence at Great Munden!

In fact, *Hertfordshire Privies* has ended up offering rather more than 'a nostalgic trip down the garden path'. From chapters covering wider lavatorial issues within the county, readers can also learn how the invading Romans tried to get us to clean up our act; of a Victorian ecological disaster when one town 'went on the drains'; of the urinal in a former stately home, where goldfish swim happily in its water cistern; and of the Edwardian public convenience that has been converted into an Italian restaurant.

Equally fascinating are the memories from childhood – a time when those parts of the body involved in the disposal of waste feature strongly in thoughts, words and deeds. One friend wrote of his worry that I was planning to reveal the identity of the phantom writer who chalked 'BUM' on a wall at the Sacred Heart Convent at Hitchin, prompting a minor witch-hunt by the nuns. We were six at the time and I was an accomplice. Don't worry Peter, your secret's safe with me!

A more official sign, which really *did* strike the fear of God in me, was the one on the wall of a foul-smelling gents' urinal in the town. It read:

TO PREVENT CONSUMPTION DO NOT SPIT.

Yes! It's a three-holer! The author at Brockholds Farm, Great Munden.

An attempt by some wag to change the P of SPIT into an H did nothing to lessen the terrifying thought that I might be inhaling deadly tuberculosis germs because some idiot hadn't heeded the sign. So the only safe course had been to hold my breath as I spent my penny.

Defecation in less-than-private surroundings can be embarrassing too – as I learned during my years with the Grammar School scout troop. Following the instructions set out by our leader Lord Baden-Powell in *Scouting for Boys*, our first job on setting up camp was to dig the latrine. A trench two feet deep, three or four feet long and only a foot wide. That way, users could perform by squatting astride it and then cover their deposit with a spadeful of earth. Although the latrine was 'concealed' by a flimsy hessian screen one still felt very public, especially when a less-inhibited boy arrived and asked you to 'move up a bit' so he could share the trench.

The pursuit of scatology cannot be classified as the most romantic of pastimes, yet the subject of where to do it and what to do with it afterwards has fascinated people right down the centuries, to the present time with the problems of 'waste management' that face our astronauts. It is a common denominator of the human race that ignores class, colour and religion. Few people ever forget their own moments of crisis in these matters. The times they were 'caught short' or the day the drains became blocked.

When we lived in the village of Pirton during the 1960s, the ancient drains serving our Elizabethan cottage were causing so many problems that I decided to buy a set of drain rods. As news of this investment spread, my services were soon in demand all round the village green. One emergency occurred on Christmas Day just as our family and guests were finishing lunch. My friend John has never forgotten the experience as he and I – still sporting our paper hats – worked the rods back and forth to clear the blockage. Puffing on cigars to cover the smell, we paused occasionally to take a swig from the glass of whisky we had each taken with us. Such experiences enable me to assure the reader that *Hertfordshire Privies* is written by someone who knows his stuff – and a lot of other people's as well!

When he heard of my appeal for privy stories a former BBC colleague reminded me of an earlier indication of my suitability to write about matters lavatorial. In the newsroom one evening years ago, when scripts were still produced on stencils by a team of typists, their shift-leader suddenly uttered a little scream and turned bright pink. She then dashed round the newsroom collecting up copies of the programme's title page, which she tore up and consigned to the waste bin. Only later was she persuaded to reveal the reason for her panic. As touch-typists will know, the W and S keys are struck with the same finger of the left hand. On this occasion a finger had strayed, with the result that the BBC's *Nine O'Clock News* was due to be read that evening by Richard Shitmore!

RICHARD WHITMORE

[1]

DAYS OF OLD

In days of old
When knights were bold
And paper wasn't invented,
They wiped their arse
On blades of grass
And went to war contented.

When it comes to the history of sanitary engineering, Britain can hardly claim to have led the world. 'Bringing up the rear' might be a better description. For many of the plumbing and sewage disposal systems that we proudly 'introduced' in Victorian times had been invented and put to good use by the Greeks, the Egyptians and other civilisations thousands of years earlier.

The Roman invaders did their best to educate us in these matters. Thanks to them, some residents of the future county of Hertfordshire enjoyed the benefits of piped water, lavatories and sewage disposal systems as early as the 2nd and 3rd centuries AD. Outstanding examples of this work came to light at St Albans during excavations on the site of the Roman city of Verulamium in the 1950s.

In the remains of a large house close to the Forum and busy Watling Street, traces of two latrines were found; one a two-seater, the other apparently able to accommodate up to 20 people at a time. Archaeologists believe the larger one catered for both sexes and may have been run by the house's owner as a business enterprise for travellers and people visiting the market. The county's first purpose-built public convenience, perhaps?

The lavatory itself was probably quite luxurious, with stone or even marble seats under which ran troughs of flowing water that washed the solids away through a three-foot sewer pipe to the River Ver. Not all the houses of Verulamium would have been served by the sewer network, though. The poorer families would have had to carry their slops and sewage to a neighbourhood cesspit while the less considerate simply emptied their earthenware chamber pots out of the window into the street.

Any story of Romano-British hygiene in Hertfordshire must include the unique display that lies in a protective vault nine metres below motorway traffic on the A1(M) at Welwyn. In 1960, a local archaeologist, Tony Rook, spotted a Roman tile projecting from the mud on the banks of the River Mimram, just a few hundred yards from Welwyn village. Excavations by Mr Rook and his colleagues revealed what's now known as the Dicket Mead Villa, a farmstead built in the 3rd century AD and which features a particularly well-preserved example of a bath house.

In Roman times, bathing was an important social function at which guests would be entertained with music and poetry and where business transactions were often done. As with present-day Turkish Baths, the bathing included massage and oiling, followed by progress through several rooms of increasing heat during which the bather would use a curved blade-like instrument called a strigil to scrape away dirt released by the perspiration and oil. This operation would be followed by a rinse in the hot bath before returning back through the cooler rooms to end the session with a cold plunge. The Welwyn ruins provide a clear picture of this process, which is why the decision was taken to go to some expense to protect this important part of the Dicket Mead excavation for present and future generations to visit and admire.

Unfortunately, all those years of Roman health education had little effect on the rough lot that followed. As the

The Roman Bath House entrance at Welwyn, preserved in steel under the
A1(M).

A view showing something of the elaborate foundations of the Roman Bath House. (*Welwyn and Hatfield Museum Service*)

Romans departed and the Anglo-Saxons arrived, most people slipped back into their dirty ways.

In castles, *garderobes* – as the privies were known – were built into the thick stone walls but nobody seemed to worry where the sewage ended up. These toilets usually consisted of a row of up to four very basic seats fixed over a shaft, down which the waste plummeted to end up in a cesspit or, more often, in the stinking moat that surrounded the fortress. At some castles, the waste simply poured out of a vent and was left to run down the outside wall.

The garderobe system was also used in private houses, such as 'Amores', a medieval hall house at Hertingfordbury. The timbered garderobe extension and window, which can be seen adjoining the chimney stack, was added in the 1540s by William North, a wealthy merchant. North had the garderobe built to adjoin the main bedroom where it was later converted into a fireside cupboard. The original soil

The timbered garderobe extension at Amores, Hertingfordbury.

The door to the garderobe in the main bedroom at Amores.

shaft still exists below the floorboards.

The monks were the first to realise the importance of having a system of pipes and flowing water to flush body waste away from their monasteries. They achieved it either by digging canals to divert water from nearby rivers or by trapping rain water from the monastery roof and storing it in tanks above the privies – or reredorters – that adjoined each dormitory. The Abbot of St Albans is on record as having built a stone cistern for rain water to flush his personal lavatory in the early part of the 12th century – which puts him in the running as the first Englishman to have a flushing water closet, albeit a primitive one.

In 1924 another interesting clue to the sanitary habits of the St Albans monks was unearthed during an excavation of the Great Cloister, adjacent to the city's cathedral. This revealed a cesspit from the original monastery and Mr H.A.J. Lamb, writing later in the *Architects' Journal*, reported, 'At the bottom were found pieces of pottery and fragments of coarse cloth which, it is thought, were old gowns torn up by the monks and used as toilet paper. Evidence that the monks suffered from digestive troubles, which were by no means rare in those days, was proved by finding in the pit seeds of the blackthorn – a powerful aperient.'

Although hygiene standards *within* the monasteries were impressive, they still added to general pollution problems because their discharged sewage was ending up in open ditches and rivers with everyone else's. In medieval times, most public lavatories were built over rivers, and since all sorts of other waste material was thrown into the water as well it led to many becoming choked with all manner of foul rubbish, ranging from human excrement to rotting animal entrails.

Eventually, communities were forced to bring in laws to clean up their surroundings. It became an offence to dump refuse in the street. Street cleaners, or 'scavengers', began appearing and communal cesspits were provided as places for householders to empty their privies. Naturally, the pits themselves had to be emptied from time to time and the men who performed this unsavoury work were known as rakers or gongfermors – from the Saxon words gong (to go off) and fey (to cleanse). Their pay of between 20 and 40 shillings a pit, depending on the size, would have been considered a small fortune at the time. Yet they must have earned every penny of it, for their equipment was very limited and there are grisly accounts of gongfermors dying horrible deaths by drowning in excrement when rotting wooden covers collapsed under their feet.

[2]

GETTING RID OF SMELLS

'I am very much offended with those Ladies, who are too proud and lazy, that they will not be at the pains of stepping into the garden to pluck a rose, but keep an odious implement, sometimes in the bed-chamber itself.'

The satirist Jonathan Swift (1667–1745) was clearly disgusted by those women who refused to make a trip to the outside privy to 'pluck a rose' – as the act of defecation was politely described in Georgian society. In a pamphlet *Directions to Servants* he went on to advise those who had to empty the offending pans to have no qualms about shaming thoughtless mistresses into cleaner habits:

'... and you are the usual carriers away of the pan, which maketh not only the chamber but even their clothes offensive, to all who come near. Now, to cure them of the odious practice, let me advise you, on whom this office lieth to convey away this utensil, that you will do it openly, down the great stairs, and in the presence of the footmen: and, if anybody knocketh, to open the street door while you have the vessel in your hands: this, if anything will make your lady take the pains of evacuating her person in the proper place, rather than expose her filthiness to all the men servants in the house.'

It was all very well for famous names like Chippendale and Sheraton to produce grand pieces of furniture designed specifically to conceal these receptacles; but the most elegant commode in the world could do nothing to disguise the

Early ceramic lavatory bowls at the Museum of St Albans.

pong if anything more than a penny was spent in it.

Back in the 16th century, it was the odour factor that had prompted Sir John Harington, godson of Queen Elizabeth I, to invent a form of flush toilet for his house at Kelstone, near Bath. Up to this time, royalty and the nobility favoured what were known as 'close stools'. These elegant, velvet-covered chests with a hole in the top and a bucket inside looked splendid but smelt as foul as any humble chamber pot.

Consequently, the success of Sir John's flushing loo led to a royal command for a similar one to be installed at Richmond Palace for his illustrious godmother. But that was all. Nobody else appeared to be interested. The *hoi polloi* couldn't afford one anyway and the nobility – with numerous servants of the bed-chamber to empty their close stools for them – saw no reason to change the habits of a lifetime. After Sir John's invention, there's no mention of another royal water closet until the early 18th century when Queen Anne had one installed adjoining her dressing room at Windsor Castle: 'A little place with a seat of easement of marble, with sluices of water to wash all down.'

By the end of the 1700s, nasty house smells began to disappear following the invention of the all-important S-bend water trap, which prevents foul air from returning back up the lavatory and into the room. The first of these was designed by Alexander Cummings, a watch and clockmaker. Shortly after his came an improved version by Thomas Prosser and finally (in 1778) one designed by Joseph Bramah, whose model set the pattern of ceramic lavatories for the next 100 years. By 1797, his factory had sold 6,000 WCs. Their craftsmanship and efficiency were considered so high that it resulted in a new slang word being added to the English language – something of outstanding quality being 'really bramah'. Even then it was to be many years before such lavatories became a standard feature of every home.

The Museum of St Albans has some good examples of

A rear view of Moule's earth closet, showing the hopper and bucket.

early ceramic lavatory bowls. One, which is mid-19th century, had no S-bend and emptied straight down a pipe into the house cesspit, which meant that foul air came straight back into the room. Another is a later Victorian design incorporating an S-bend water trap which prevented smells from returning. These two bowls were not considered particularly ornate in their time – the really posh ones had highly-decorated relief mouldings on the *outside* as well!

Another important Victorian invention that did much to get rid of smells was the kind of toilet remembered by Bert Hosier of Northchurch, near Berkhamsted: 'We had an outside lavatory in a tin hut way down the garden, where the pull of the handle delivered not a flush of water but a measured amount of sawdust or ashes. . .'

This was an updated version of the earth closet, developed by the Reverend Henry Moule (1801–1880) and which in its day made quite a lot of sense. Mr Moule, who was Vicar of Fordington in Dorset, argued that water was the wrong way to dispose of human excrement. It neither absorbed nor deodorised. It was merely 'a vehicle' for moving the stuff off the premises and depositing it in a cesspool. Having decided that the stench of his own cesspool was offending the neighbours he had it filled in and told his family that they would be using buckets in future. Later, when he buried their droppings in the garden he discovered that, within a month, not a trace could be found. His next move was to build an outside privy where the contents of the bucket were mixed with dry earth from the privy floor.

'The whole operation does not take a boy more than a quarter of an hour,' he wrote. 'And, within ten minutes after its completion, neither the eye nor nose can perceive anything offensive.' Not only that, the human manure produced a 'luxuriant growth of vegetables' in the vicarage garden. Encouraged by these experiments, Moule set about designing his first earth closet.

Like the privy, it had a hinged seat over a bucket. However, in the unit behind was a hopper filled with dry earth, ashes or charcoal which could be released into the bucket in measured amounts by pulling a handle. This eliminated smells and the problem of flies. The hopper held sufficient earth for about 25 visits, which meant that a closet serving a family of six would get through about two-and-a-half tons of earth every year.

After successful trials, the scatological Vicar of Fordington took out patents and founded the Moule Patent Earth-Closet Company Ltd, which was soon doing brisk business.

As the vicar's company flourished, more sophisticated earth closets began to appear. One, in an expensive mahogany cabinet, boasted an automatic earth-release mechanism, based on pressure, which went into action as soon as the user's bottom rose from the seat!

The Reverend Moule believed his invention would become the lavatory of the future and spent the rest of his life trying to convince a sceptical government of the need to adopt a national policy to encourage the use of earth closets. Quite how they would have worked in the built-up areas of our towns and cities he never explained.

Nevertheless, his invention made a valuable contribution to the health and hygiene of the nation at a time when the authorities were still striving to perfect that most important advance in the history of human health – keeping our excrement out of our drinking water. But providing supplies of pure piped water and efficient systems of sewage disposal and treatment were a long time coming because they cost a great deal of money. In this respect Hertfordshire, like every other county, had its triumphs and its disasters.

The curator of Hitchin Museum, Isabel Wilson, showing how the user would have to lift a handle to release the measured amount of earth into the bucket.

A close up of the handle. This earth closet came originally from the Old Forge at Weston.

[3]

HEALTH, CONVENIENCE AND 'A GREAT PRIVY'

Amwell, perpetual be thy stream
Nor, e'er thy springs be less
Which thousands drink who never dream
Whence flows the boon they bless.

This verse is from a short poem that commemorates an adventurous 17th-century project, begun at Great Amwell in Hertfordshire, to bring better hygiene to the people of London. Even though sewage was still flowing in open ditches in many places, progress in other aspects of urban sanitation was beginning to happen. One of the biggest health risks in the fast-growing cities was the fact that water supplies that had served each district for centuries were no longer able to keep up with demand. So plans had to be drawn up to bring fresh water in from the surrounding countryside.

In 1609, our county became the focal point of one of the earliest schemes to boost fresh water supplies to England's capital. It was the inspiration of Hugh Myddelton, an MP and wealthy gold bullion merchant, who financed and supervised the construction of a canal known as the New River. Still flowing today, the man-made waterway begins at springs in the Great Amwell area, near Ware. When first opened, it wound its way for nearly 40 miles to a reservoir in Clerkenwell, from where the water was distributed to several north London districts through wooden pipes made from hollowed-out tree trunks.

Myddelton's scheme, which took four years to complete, nearly foundered when his company ran out of funds as the aqueduct reached Enfield. However, such was its importance

This display of early sanitary ware at the Museum of St Albans includes a section of the wooden piping used in the New River project, on the wall beside the curator, Ann Roach.

The Great Amwell springs today.

that King James I ordered the Treasury to make a grant of £8,600 to guarantee its completion. The project, which runs parallel to the River Lea for much of the way, earned its developer a knighthood.

The Great Amwell springs were later laid out with islands by a local benefactor, who also had monuments erected to commemorate Sir Hugh's achievement in 'conveying health, pleasure and convenience to the Metropolis of Great Britain.'

Two centuries later another scheme, to bring 'health and convenience' to a Hertfordshire town, had a less triumphant outcome. With the passing of the Public Health Act of 1848 it became compulsory for every household to have access to a fixed sanitary arrangement of one kind or another and a clean supply of water from the town water works. The market town of Hitchin, then the largest community in north Hertfordshire, was among the first to adopt the Act but their

26

calamitous efforts to get 'on the drains' produced a series of financial crises and environmental disasters that took several decades to put right.

The town had been placed under a Public Health order following local petitions and a visit from an inspector of the General Board of Health, who found 400 residents suffering from typhoid. Hardly surprising, perhaps, when half the 1,200 homes were drawing their water from 92 different wells, many of which were polluted. He also found the condition of most privies in the town 'unspeakable', mainly because there were far too few for the number of people using them.

By 1850 a local Board of Health was elected to put things right. They began well enough. The River Hiz, which flows through the town, was cleaned and a mile of trunk sewer laid under the river bed. To this were connected some ten miles of street drains and relevant branch pipes. Then, in May 1853, when everything was in readiness for connection to individual properties, the Board ran into serious financial difficulties. Costs had soared to £4,000 above the original estimates and no means of purifying the raw sewage had yet been provided.

By 1854 a water supply had been laid to about 400 properties but the pumping station kept breaking down, resulting in water cuts. Then it was discovered that the recently-laid trunk sewer was defective and leaking. The climax to this series of disasters came in 1857. A heavy storm caused water in the main sewer to rise so high that it backed up into the pump house reservoir, with the result that some householders found sewage coming out of their domestic taps!

In the meantime, a miller brought a claim for damages against the Board of Health for allowing sewage to pollute the river that powered his water-wheel. Joshua Ransom, who supplied much of the town's bread from Grove Mill on the

This photo of Grove Mill and Joshua Ransom's house shows the close proximity of the millhead pool that became polluted with raw sewage. *(Hitchin Museum)*

outskirts of Hitchin, claimed his premises had been 'converted into a great privy' and the millhead pool 'into a disgusting cesspool from the filth deposited along the bed, from which arise millions of bubbles constantly discharging their mephitic gas and giving it the appearance of being in a permanent state of fermentation.'

Mr Ransom's claim for damages was eventually upheld but the Board of Health disbanded sooner than face the financial consequences and it wasn't until 1870 that a new Board was elected to set matters right. It took them 20 years to clear the debts amassed by their predecessors and it was the turn of the century before Hitchin obtained its first proper sewage treatment works. This still functions today, at Bury Mead, close by the old Grove Mill site.

One of the biggest health threats to towns came from the densely-packed slum areas, most of which had been built by

Hitchin's first sewage works under construction at Bury Mead in 1910.

property speculators during the early part of the 19th century. Hundreds of poorly-constructed 'one up, one down' cottages were crammed into inn yards, gardens and any other available space close to the main thoroughfare. Apart from a small fireplace in the downstairs room they had no other facility. Water came from a communal well or pump and the only lavatories were one or two privies at the far end of the yard.

Haydens Court, off Railway Street, Hertford, was one such area. A report in 1850 said there were eleven cottages with 27 occupants and only two privies to serve them. These privies stood over an ash pit but others in the town were discharging straight into the River Lea. In the photograph, the Haydens Court privy shed can be seen at the far end. By 1933, it had been fitted with three flush toilets. But according to Les Sullivan (the small boy sitting on the doorstep nearest the camera) water still had to be fetched from a communal tap

29

Haydens Court, Hertford in 1933. *(Hertford Museum)*

and there were no sinks in the houses. All the washing – clothes and people – was done in the tin bath that is hanging on the wall.

Similarly, in 1850, Hertford's Dolphin Yard had six properties tenanted by 24 people and 'one privy over a dunghill'. In 1893 it was still 'in an unsanitary state' but ten years later the little cottages were on mains water and the privies seen in the photograph had been connected to the main sewer. Mrs Elsie Hockley, who grew up in Oakers Buildings, a similar yard off St Andrew's Street, said they had six communal toilets to serve 17 houses. However, only the first one had a flush cistern, so the water from that one had to clean the gulley for the other five toilets at the same time.

The 1848 Act had been greeted with fierce opposition by the slum landlords – who could see their profits diminishing – and by other ratepayers who feared the improvements recommended by the government's health inspectors would

Dolphin Yard, Hertford. *(Hertford Museum)*

put their community in heavy debt for many years. Watford was no exception, as an anonymous handbill, makes clear (see bottom of page 34).

At this time, the 'town hamlet of Watford', as it was described in the inspector's report, had a population of about 5,000 which had been rising steadily because of a heavy influx of navvies employed on the construction of the London to Birmingham Railway. This had resulted in severe overcrowding in the slum courts which, in turn, put pressure on the primitive drainage system. Nearly all of these courts and alleys led off the High Street – and that was where much of the sewage ended up. A situation vividly described in the report of Health Inspector, George Clark Esq, following his visit in 1849.

'There are no efficient sewers in the town. Down the main street on either side of the road is an open gutter . . . uncovered drains cross the footway and, flowing down from the side courts, convey the overflow of cesspools and the offal of slaughterhouses . . . There are six principal slaughterhouses, for the most part in the most crowded and filthiest alleys in the town. It is also a common custom with those who keep pigs to kill the animals in the sty. These pig sties are very numerous and are chiefly found in the worst parts of the town . . . Houses below The Dog public house have privies with open cess pools, pig sties, dungheaps and are without drains. The house slops are for the most part thrown into the main road and public footway which, at the time of my visit, was in a state very offensive to passers-by. This is a fever locality.'

One of the main complaints made to Mr Clark was about the hardness of the well water. 'From various statements made to me on the spot, it appears that the want of soft water is severely felt by the poor. One woman, though so poor as to receive relief from the parish, yet finds it worth-while to pay a boy 2d weekly to fetch river water when her rain-water store

The rear of Ballards Buildings, Watford's most notorious slum court. In 1853 the Local Board of Health estimated that between 300 and 400 people were occupying the 39 cottages and lodging houses at any one time. In the foreground are the row of privies that served the occupants at the time of the courtyard's demolition in 1926.*(Photo courtesy of Kimberley Bowen)*

fails, as it does for nine months of the year. Others complained of the increased consumption of soda and soap . . . This is unusually great; 6d or 7d a week does not appear an extraordinary payment per family for these articles.'

Despite 'the spirit of dissention' noted in Mr Clark's report, a Local Board of Health was established in Watford a year later but real progress was painfully slow. As with Hitchin to the north, the Local Board tried to keep costs down by using cheap labour and materials – which resulted in more problems. Slum landlords did no more than they needed to 'improve' the overcrowded courts and alleys, many of which remained until well into the 20th century.

TO THE

Inhabitants of Watford.

A PUBLIC

MEETING

WILL BE HELD AT THE

George Inn, Watford,

On Friday, 2nd day of March, 1849, at 11 o'Clock, for the purpose of taking into consideration the contemplated

SERIOUS OUTLAY

UNDER THE

Health of Towns Bill.

It is particularly urged that the Ratepayers should attend, and look to their own Interests by opposing the Proceedings now being carried on ; which will entail an enormous expense that cannot be liquidated for many years.

A RATEPAYER.

Watford, Feb. 28th, 1848.

PEACOCK, PRINTER, WATFORD

---

[4]

'A PRIVATE PLACE OF EASE'

A privy hole is deep and vast
Of unknown depths beware.
Both hands must clasp the board quite fast
Or greet its murky lair.

So, brimming over with facts from Hertfordshire's wide-ranging history of sanitation, we reach the main topic of this book. The eponymous privy. The little building that stood at the end of the garden path, or across the yard, and was the standard lavatory for most people in the county until the first half of the 20th century.

I quickly learned that those indulging in the sport of privy hunting should be constantly prepared for surprises. What has amazed me is how many 'bucket-and-chuck-its' were still in use during the *second* half of the century. As the following stories will reveal, many were functioning throughout the 1950s and early 1960s – especially in the villages and hamlets of north and east Hertfordshire.

For a long time I thought the title for 'Most Recently Occupied Privy' would be held by the Cunninghams of Great Munden, who moved to a derelict farmhouse in 1983 and found themselves having to use a garden privy while proper sanitary fittings were being installed. Then, I received a letter from Mrs Rita Dedman who revealed that in 1986, when she and her family moved into a cottage by the side of the A10 at Wadesmill, near Ware, she was astonished to discover that her late neighbours – an elderly brother and sister – had an outside bucket toilet which was in use until 1990! Surely a record?

Not so. Just one week before I finished this book I called in

The privy at Pirton Grange.

The night soil door in the wall of the Pirton privy.

on Pirton Grange, a 15th-century moated farmhouse just north of Hitchin near the Bedfordshire border. This historic house, home of the Handscombe farming family for 400 years, had been sold at auction in 1996 but needed a vast amount of restoration work to make it habitable.

Having discovered that the new owners, Jim and Mary Moffatt, had already stripped out the old lavatories, I was about to leave, when Mrs Moffatt added: 'Of course, we still have an outside privy if you're interested but I need to check first – because it's still being used by the workmen!'

And there it was! The ultimate find! An original farmhouse box-and-bucket privy from Victorian, possibly Georgian, times still intact – and in use! Still with its original well-scrubbed seat and the nightsoil door in the wall behind. Unchallengable winner of the title – 'Hertfordshire's Most Recently Occupied Privy!'

37

The Mill Green privy – and bucket!

The word privy – 'A private place of ease; a latrine' – is thought to be 600 years old and comes from the Latin word *privatus* meaning apart or secret. In times past it was the standard word for the lavatory, but has always been associated more with the little brick or wooden building that stood apart from the main house. Over the years it has acquired a great number of euphemisms. Some of these crop up in the following chapters and, for really keen students, a full (but not necessarily complete) list is provided at the end of the book.

Of those privies that feature in the following pages most have been out of use for many years but have somehow survived. One of the best-preserved of the wooden ones stands in the garden of Mill Green Museum at Hatfield. It once served cottages on the Marquess of Salisbury's estate.

Here are two unadorned descriptions of privies as remembered by folk who once used them. The first came from Mr Cyril Martin, of Park Street, near St Albans: 'I was born in 1904. I lived in one of a block of five workman's cottages. The privies were situated at a point in the back garden furthest away from the cottages. Each had a wooden door furnished with an iron opening latch mounted on the inside. The latch could be operated from the outside by putting your finger through a hole in the door. When inside, privacy could be obtained by sliding a small wooden shutter over the hole.

'Facing the door was the box-like wooden seat with the very necessary hole in the centre. The whole plumbed an iron bucket standing beneath. There was a suitably-sized wooden door in the back of the privy to allow the bucket to be inserted or withdrawn. Our privies were used mostly by the wives and children of the cottages as the men had to leave home early and walk long distances away. . .'

From across the other side of the county, Mr John Drage of Therfield, near Royston, wrote:

Mr and Mrs Godfrey-Evans of Wheathampstead with their 18th-century privy.

'Seats were kept well-scrubbed or even painted. The walls were whitewashed or distempered and I once saw one that had been wallpapered. My late great-aunt had an advert for Pears soap pinned to the wall, with the Pears boy on it blowing soap bubbles. Others I remember had small pictures on the wall. One would usually find a can of disinfectant behind the door – and always a pad of newspaper cut in neat squares, hanging on a nail.'

At Bury Farm Cottage, Wheathampstead, David and Ann Godfrey-Evans have an 18th-century red brick privy built against an ancient flint wall. Their property was owned by Westminster Abbey until 1945, which may explain the unusually high quality of workmanship that went into the building, with its solid wooden door and brick floor. The thunderbox itself is long gone and the privy, like most that have survived, is now used as a store.

Domestic privies took two basic forms. Those that

contained a bucket, like the one at Bury Farm Cottage, and those with a brick-lined or concreted pit beneath the wooden box. Privies with a pit were emptied only two or three times a year, depending on the size of the family. Some were designed so that the pit projected out of the back of the building. Inside smells were thus kept to a minimum and the pit could be emptied without causing too much disturbance.

Pit emptying was carried out by a modern equivalent of the medieval 'gongfermor'. In the 18th and 19th centuries he was described in official documents as 'the necessary man' – 'the necessary' being one of the most popular euphemisms for the privy. One Thomas Draper is listed as the necessary man on the Marquess of Salisbury's estate at Hatfield during the 18th century.

In many parts of the county these gentlemen were more affectionately known as 'the lavender men'. They went about their duties with a smelly horse-drawn metal cart and armed with a 'shit-scoop' – a substantial metal bowl with a six-foot wooden handle which they used to ladle the sewage out of the privy and into a bucket for transfer to the cart. According to Margaret Day of Flamstead, it was the local coalman who did the job in her village. He was still collecting privy waste in his big bins right up to the 1950s. Where Mrs Lesley Rome of Hitchin grew up, privies were known as dunnakins and the young man who emptied them was called Dunnakin John. 'You could smell him coming from miles away!' she says.

Such men were held in high regard by those who relied on their services. Bottles of beer and other gifts would be left out for them when they were due to call. The job was often done at night, when sleeping families were less likely to be disturbed by the stench from the lavender cart. Thus, the contents of the buckets became known as 'nightsoil' and the door in the privy through which the buckets could be retrieved became 'the nightsoil door'.

Barry Goodall of Letchworth recalled a childhood jingle that captures the cheeky curiosity of youngsters as they peeped through the bedroom curtains to watch the contents of their privy being tipped into the horse-drawn cart, before it trundled away on its nocturnal journey:

> The nightsoil men turn out at ten
> Their picks and shovels with'em;
> They have a big light
> And shovel out the shite,
> Hoorah for the nightsoil men!

Privy buckets were designed with a longer handle than ordinary buckets so that they could be carried and emptied without the contents slopping over the hands and feet. One belonging to Arthur Bird of Manuden near Bishops Stortford, was in use until 1962, when his cottage was linked to the village's main sewer. Until then the bucket was emptied down the garden late at night when all the neighbours were indoors.

Many householders (like the Reverend Moule of earth-closet fame) believed the contents of their privy bucket made an invaluable contribution to the garden. Hazel Frost of Hitchin remembers relatives who had a privy that actually formed part of the house and had a nightsoil door in the outside wall. Her husband's uncle always used the contents to obtain excellent results from his vegetable plot. Apparently, he never had to buy any tomato or cucumber plants because so many grew each year from the pips that had recently passed through his family!

At the start of this century, the health authorities were still having terrible problems persuading residents and local councils of the urgent need to spend more money providing better household drains and proper sewage disposal plants. In 1904 one of Hertfordshire's exasperated medical officers,

Arthur Bird's privy bucket.

a Dr Day, reported: 'The larger villages such as Graveley, Offley, Pirton, Weston and Wymondley possess a sewer in its most primitive form, more or less an open ditch which takes the refuse water beyond the confines of the village. In Weston the ditch is only a few feet from a row of cottages.'

Elsewhere there were reports that street sewers in the biggest villages, Codicote, Ickleford, Whitwell and Kimpton were producing 'a particularly offensive stench' in warm weather. By the 1930s, things had improved and in 1933 the medical officer for Welwyn Rural District, Mr H.W. Grattan, was able to report that his council 'no longer had to undertake the emptying of earth closets and cesspools.'

But it was not just the cost that made some householders reluctant to have flush toilets inside their homes. Brenda Cook of St Albans tells how, in 1914, her father William went to see his grandmother and Aunt Liz, who lived at Codicote. At the time, Aunt Liz was full of the fact that a neighbour had just had a lavatory (presumably a water closet) built adjoining the kitchen. Mr Cook, then a boy of seven, remembers the strong feelings of disgust expressed by his aunt at the idea of placing a human waste disposal unit so close to the area of the house where food was prepared. 'Maybe she had a point,' says Brenda.

A story matched by a lady from Berkhamsted who wrote about her 93 year old aunt who lived in a cottage and had used an outside loo all her life. When younger neighbours moved in next door, they installed a modern flush toilet, leaving the bucket privy abandoned down the garden path. The aged aunt was heard to remark: 'They're using that inside lav all the time now, the dirty devils!'

[5]

DOWN THE BLACK HOLE!

A Hertfordshire schoolboy named Hyde
Fell into the privy and died.
Then his young brother
Fell into the other
And now they're interred, side by side.

Long dark walks down the garden path and a horror of accidentally slipping off the seat into the black hole of the big wooden box. These are the two most vivid childhood memories of that last generation for whom the privy was once a part of everyday life. It is interesting that nearly all those who have contributed their recollections for this book knew exactly how many paces the family privy stood from the back door; conjuring up pictures of little figures in nightwear clutching a torch or a jam jar with a candle in it and counting 'twenty seven, twenty eight, twenty nine...' under their breath as they scampered on their scary nocturnal trips to and from the wooden shed at the bottom of the garden.

A privy with a two-sized double seat for adult and child is the sole survivor of several that served Cold Christmas Cottages at Thundridge, near Ware. Now classified as a listed building, it is 'listing' somewhat itself, under the weight of the ivy that has grown over it. Like most others, the privy stands at the far end of the garden, 35 yards from the cottage – not a nice trip for a child on a cold winter's night.

Few could have had a worse trip than young Harold Woods, now of Letchworth, who was one of a family of seven who grew up in a tiny cottage at Cromer, near Stevenage: 'Our privy was situated some 60 or 70 yards away, at the

The Cold Christmas two-seater.

furthermost boundary of the vegetable garden, where it adjoined the farmer's pond. At some stage prior to my appearance a chapel was built on part of the garden, thus separating us from our little hut.

'Try to imagine a seven year old, troubled with a bilious attack, being forced to go at three o'clock on a January morning with six inches of snow on the ground. . . . Fumbling around in the darkness for clothes, creeping downstairs and having to set off through the snow. Round the chapel and past the pond to the Haven of Relief, with its frozen latch and very cold seat. That was 1927 but it could just as well have been 1827!'

Equally vivid memories came from Margaret Day, of Flamstead, near St Albans, who still lives in the cottage where she grew up and who had to use chamber pots and a bucket toilet until the 1950s. The 'country seat' (as the family called it) was in a shed at the far end of their yard, backing onto the cemetery. 'As a child, I remember being very frightened on dark nights, especially when the branches of the churchyard trees scraped on the privy's corrugated iron roof. It gave me the creeps and I would sit there too frightened to move until I heard Mum or Dad call out "Have you taken root in there?" Then I would shoot back across the yard into the house.'

For a while, Margaret and her family also had to cope with the problem of Perky, a handsome but very aggressive black cockerel that they adopted. Their privy door had a small hole cut in it so that the cat could shelter inside during bad weather. When Perky discovered this, he promptly took over the privy and refused to allow anyone in.

'The cat was terrified of him,' Margaret recalled. 'Perky would sit inside the toilet and peck at anybody that tried to go in. Then, when he grew too big to get through the cat hole, he would lie in wait outside and have a go at us as we left. It got to the stage where we had to arm ourselves with a rolled-up newspaper to beat off his attacks.'

Margaret Day with the washstand and chamber pot from her childhood days at Pound Cottage, Flamstead.

Rita Dedman of Wadesmill near Ware, had more daunting birds to negotiate. During her wartime childhood in Cheshunt the family had a proper flushing loo but that, too, was down the garden. To reach it, she had to get past about a dozen free-range geese which always chased her. 'I shall never forget those walks down to the bottom of what seemed then a mile-long garden,' she wrote. 'Sometimes I had to take a candle as there was no electric light; with a coat over one's head in the bad weather. Oh! What wonderful years!'

Others had four-legged creatures to worry about, like the one that gave Kathleen Filby of Braughing her fear of using the privy on her grandfather's farm: 'It had a scrubbed wooden seat with two holes, one small and one large for child and adult. I hardly dare mention that an aunt was sitting there once, when a rat jumped out of the smaller hole!' Similar nightmarish images came from John Drage of Therfield: 'Those privies with a wooden floor were a popular place for rats to make their nests and it wasn't unknown for one to appear while you were sitting there. So it became the golden rule that, every time you went, you stamped your foot on the floor on entry!'

John also had a lighter memory from his 'privy days' – the unchanging daily routine of an uncle who lived next door. 'On his way to the glory hole each morning he would remove his leather belt and hang it round his neck and then sing a verse from *Onward Christian Soldiers* as he walked the 25 yards down the garden path.'

Young ladies from the towns, who were accustomed to flushing toilets, never forgot the culture shock when confronted by their first rural thunder box and bucket. Joan Standingford, of Stevenage, had to use one during a visit to her uncle's thatched cottage in Pirton in the 1920s: 'I was rather aghast when my mother said she had better come with me, because I was quite capable of going by myself. However, after walking through a long passage we finally came to the end of the building – and there was this monstrosity in front of me, going right across the room! It was made of wood, with a small hole for children and a bigger one for adults.

'I felt quite honoured when I had to climb up a step to reach the hole – like a queen sitting on a throne. I well remember thinking at the time what a good job I sat on the little one, as I had visions of disappearing down the big hole into – well, I really don't know where! I was absolutely horrified when I discovered that there wasn't a chain!'

Even more vivid are the war-time 'loo' memories of Mrs Millie Lisser from Hitchin who, as a schoolgirl of 14, was evacuated to Hertfordshire with her family: 'In 1940, at the height of the blitz, we left our house in Stoke Newington and found ourselves billeted in a remote farmhouse near Codicote with two other families. At one point, four of us were living in one room, cooking on an open fire. The house was lit by oil lamps because there was no gas or eletricity. It was the first time I had been unable to have a proper bath because the water supply came from a well in the yard.

'It was a bitterly cold winter and the only toilet (serving four families) was a brick privy, situated across the farmyard next to the hen house. When it was raining or snowing you had to take an umbrella because slates were missing from the privy roof and the water poured in. We must have presented a comical sight, sitting there on the big wooden box. Believe me it's not easy to go to the loo and hold an umbrella over your head at the same time!'

In contrast, a lady from Berkhamsted says that as she trips to the toilet across plush carpet she still has fond memories of 'that long ago little house in the garden.' Her description of summertime visits grows quite lyrical: 'Our toilet was brick-built and only half-way up the garden. Numerous trips to this little house brought one closely into contact with the changing seasons. In summer I would sit with the door open and gaze across the valley of Berkhamsted, soaking in the distant view of the opposite hill encompassing Gravel Path and Sunnyside Church. . .

'Trips after dark were not such pleasing events – made with the aid of a torch and after pleading with an adult to come and wait outside. If the night was cold and crisp or, even worse, wet this companion would become very impatient! When we moved to the cottage in 1935 we inherited a toilet sitting in a scrubbed, bleached wooden box seat which spread from wall to wall – very useful for holding the accoutrements which accompanied me, as a child, on these excursions.'

A point taken up by Valerie Booth when recalling her childhood days in the family's terraced house in Copeswood Road, North Watford. Although boasting a full flushing cistern, their lavatory was situated outside, next to the coal shed. 'The pan was set in a wooden frame with a rather convenient full seat, wall-to-wall, that was most useful to place one's comics (*Dandy* and *Beano*) upon. There was also a candle in a holder for night-time usage,' Valerie says, adding that – with hindsight – the lavatory featured far more in daily life in those days.

'To keep it clean required a large bucket of hot sudsy water, a hard bristle brush and a great deal of elbow grease to scrub the wooden seating. Being wartime – hence, no wastage – the water was then poured down the pan. Even the overhead cast-iron water tank and long chain were washed over! Our little terraced house was in a block of five, all with the same lavatory systems. This led to a fine degree of neighbourliness as four out of the five houses had children. Each morning there would be a roll-call as we all trooped outside to 'go' before setting off for school. Doors were left open and gossip was exchanged and passed down the line to those unable to hear. Those bunking off school would often take their sandwiches and hide in the loo until all the adults had left for work – a system I confess to have used.'

For Valerie and her family the most memorable loo experience was the bitter winter of 1947–48 when heavy snow, followed by weeks of sub-zero temperatures, made their lavatory almost unusable. 'With snow almost three feet deep piled up against the back door and the cistern frozen solid, ingenuity was pushed to its maximum,' Valerie says. 'Hacking a pathway to the loo with shovel and yard broom, we had to drag a bucket of hot salty water to flush the frozen pan. Obviously, all this demanded excellent bladder control, as progress was slow. In the evenings we lit several candles and night-lights in the hope of de-icing the tank and pan for the next day.'

Cyril Martin had good reason for being able to recall details of the privies serving a row of cottages in the village of Park Street, where he grew up. As a boy, he suffered a lot from constipation and his mother made him spend long periods sitting in there. His school pal George, who lived next door, used to keep him amused throughout these long and boring sessions by collecting objects from the garden and holding them up in front of the privy's frosted-glass window for Cyril to try to identify.

Less innocent childhood loo games are reported by Bert Hosier in his book about growing up in the village of Northchurch, near Berkhamsted. In this, he describes the primitive toilet arrangements at the village school. The girls' lavatory consisted of a line of seats fixed over an open trough down which water flowed periodically. 'To add a little warmth to the proceedings,' says Bert, 'crumpled newspapers were sometimes lit and floated downstream with obvious results . . . whilst, in contrast, a cooling-down process sometimes occurred in the boys' roofless urinals when – over the dividing wall – it was not always rain that fell on a youthful head!'

The girls' toilet in question was probably the Trough Closet which had been produced by the famous Thomas

Crapper sanitaryware factory in Chelsea as 'an inexpensive system for schools, workhouses and factories etc.' With a large cistern at one end, sufficient water could be flushed all the way down the open trough to carry everything away. In 1902, after reports of bottom burning from various parts of the country, Mr Crapper produced an 'Improved Trough Closet Range' which made such pranks impossible.

Even so, antiquated school lavatories survived well into the 1940s in some parts of the county. Valerie Booth, remembering her war-time years in Watford, at Callowland Infants and Junior school, believes today's children would be appalled at the lack of privacy endured by youngsters of her generation. 'Situated on the far side of the playground the lavatory consisted of a bench with eight holes in it, feeding into a communal sluice. There was no proper flush system and no privacy as the cubicles had no doors. Hence one's classmates were able to observe each other as they queued in line, waiting for a cubicle,' Valerie said. 'The sluice often broke down and the caretaker had to be sent for with his high-tec equipment – a large yard broom and bucket – to get the system back into operation. This involved vacating the first cubicle so that he could start pushing the jammed effluent, while a privileged child was selected to watch at the far end of the sluice and yell "It's moving" at the appropriate time. The experience was less than fragrant in hot weather, when blow-flies could be observed at very close quarters – a world away from today!'

The final story in this little saga of schoolboy japes comes from Miss M. Hagger of Baldock, who tells how her late Uncle Ernie once extracted a satisfying revenge on his unpopular teacher after she had been giving him a hard time in class. During the break, he spotted her going into the staff privy, so he pulled up a large stinging nettle, opened the nightsoil door at the rear and pushed the nettle inside, wriggling it about until he heard a scream. By the time the lady had pulled her drawers up over her tingling bottom and emerged to look for the culprit, Ernie was across the other side of the playground playing innocently with all the other children!

[6]

'Poo Sticks and Paper'

If in here you find no paper,
Behind the door there lies a scraper.
If no scraper there be found
Wipe your arsehole on the ground!

Although the Romans used a scraper – the strigil – to remove grease and grime from their bodies while bathing, their implement for cleaning the bottom was a little kinder. It consisted of a short stick with a small sponge attached to one end. A number of these would stand in a bowl of salt water in the middle of the latrine. Afterwards, the user would clean the sponge in a shallow water channel that flowed along in front of the privy before returning the 'poo stick' to the bowl to be used again. A process, some say, that led to the expression 'getting hold of the wrong end of the stick!'

In more recent times, although lavatory paper was being manufactured in Britain back in the 1880s it wasn't until after the Second World War that it became a standard feature of household loos. Then, manufacturers like Bronco, Izal and Jeyes Hygienic used to print their motif on each sheet of the roll, to catch our eye as we sat, chin-in-hands, in meditation. In these days of multi-pack, multi-colour soft tissues, an average family will get through at least 150 rolls a year – providing the UK's bog roll industry with an annual turnover of about £600 million.

Yet many of us can still remember those days of not so long ago when even quite well-to-do families with proper flush lavatories would put their children to work on Saturday mornings making improvised 'bum fodder'. Cutting pages from the daily newspaper into neat squares, making a hole in

This illustration shows the arrangement of a Roman military Communal latrine. The sponge 'poo sticks' were kept in a bowl in the centre and legionary sitters would have running water both in front and beneath them.

one corner with a meat skewer and threading them onto a piece of string until there were sufficient for a week's supply for the nail behind the lavatory door. It was reckoned that, with care, one page of the larger broadsheet newspapers could provide 16 squares for bottom wiping.

The choice of newspapers varied from area to area and home to home. The *Daily Mail* appears to have been a popular one because the print didn't come off. In more rural parts of the county, many copies of *Farmer's Weekly* and *Farmer and Stockbreeder* ended their days behind the privy door. Because they dispensed with the chore of cutting up pages, smaller publications such as railway and bus timetables and copies of *Old Moore's Almanack* were also popular. To reduce the rough feel of the paper, privy incumbents would pass the time rubbing each page vigorously between the palms of their hands.

'Unfortunately,' writes Valerie Booth, 'the only newspaper my family took was the *Daily Mirror*.' However, so that she could stay up late and listen to Tommy Handley's radio show *I.T.M.A.*, Valerie would volunteer to sit at the table and cut old copies of the newspaper into neat squares. Then, in an effort to raise the tone slightly, she would have to thread the squares onto little strips of coloured ribbon. 'My grandmother had high standards,' she says. 'No way would we have been so common as to thread our paper onto string!' Then, on Sundays, she would go to her Granny's house – also in Watford – and repeat the process all over again. 'For this I was paid the princely sum of one shilling pocket money as she considered even that had to be earned.'

Journalist Beryl Carrington of St Albans remembers feeling very privileged because her father, who was editor of the *Hertfordshire Advertiser*, would bring home nice clean paper that had been left over from the week's printing run and therefore had no black newsprint on it to stain the bottom. Beryl adds: 'My aunt used to string up my father's weekly letters to her and my mother used to say that, on visits there, she enjoyed having a read of what he had told her about us all. . . He used violet ink, so it was all quite pretty!'

Sandra Hare, of Shillington, near Hitchin, mentions a similar privileged position enjoyed by her Nan and Grandad in the days when they had a privy. Being market gardeners, the family handled large amounts of citrus fruit – oranges, lemons and grapefruit – which would arrive individually wrapped in soft paper not unlike tissue. 'So, instead of cutting up squares of yesterday's newspaper they would carefully smooth out the wrappers and thread them onto a length of string to hang in the loo for use. The added bonus was that the fruit smell of the paper helped to hide the worst smells of the loo! When visitors commented on their posh paper, Grandad would reply, "Well we aren't tall enough to wipe our bottoms on the *Evening Star*!" As you can imagine, this raised a smile the first time you heard it but soon became a bit sad!'

Sandra also touches on the fact that, even as an adult, she found trips to outside lavatories rather daunting. 'When I first started going out with my husband his Mum gave me very strange looks when I asked if he would come and stand by the loo door when I needed to pay a visit. It was dark and eerie; owls would hoot in the walnut tree and the lilac bushes would rustle and scrape across your face as you made the journey down the windy path. I can think of better, more comfortable, seats but no doubt it was very peaceful communing with Nature in this way.'

[7]

TALES FROM THE VILLAGES

What a to-do if you have to do a poo
In an English country garden.
Pick up a leaf and wipe your underneath
In an English country garden.
(From a playground version of the popular English ballad!)

ASHWELL

Ashwell's only surviving privy was a much-travelled one
before it came to rest at Lindsay Colquhoun's home in High
Street. Having stood for years in a cottage garden elsewhere
in the village it was given a new lease of life in the 1950s when
it was acquired by a local builder, who transported it to
various sites around the district to serve the needs of his
workmen. When the firm closed down and the contents of
the builder's yard came up for sale, Lindsay felt it worth
spending a bit more than a penny to ensure that this treasure
of Ashwell's architectural heritage did not leave the village.
One wonders what his wife said when he brought it home!

Octogenarian Albert Sheldrick, who was born in the
village, told me of a certain Joe Man who used to serve his
friends a supper dish of snails that he had collected from the
walls of cottage privies in the area around Ashwell Springs.
Apparently privy snails were fatter than the others and tasted
delicious when lightly-boiled and served with salt, pepper
and a slice of bread and butter.

The springs were once famous for their watercress but a
hundred years ago this beautiful village was described by the
local Medical Officer as 'the most insanitary and disease-
ridden in the district.' One privy was found serving eight

Lindsay Colquhoun's much-travelled privy at Ashwell.

cottages, wells were contaminated with sewage and foul drains were discharging directly into the springs, 'making the water polluted before the sun has time to warm it.' A serious outbreak of typhoid in 1897 hastened plans to provide piped water, proper drainage and a sewage works but, even then, wrangling between local personalities delayed the scheme's completion for nearly 20 years.

BRAUGHING

Many privies of olden times were placed near or beneath a yew tree – in which, it was believed, the guardian angel of the resident family lived. Such is the case at the Old Vicarage at Braughing, where an ancient yew still protects this once-elegant privy – with its tiled roof and original wooden facing, cleverly made to resemble blocks of Portland stone.

The Braughing privy, under the yew tree.

Little Alice Clough and the two-holer at Braughing.

The building stands about 15 yards from the main house, which served as the vicarage to St Mary's, Braughing, until 1957. It is now occupied by the Clough family and my conducted tour of their privy, with five year old Alice Clough, revealed two single compartments (now used for storage) and a splendid two-hole ecclesiastical thunderbox, complete with lids and a door through which the soil bucket was removed for emptying.

BYGRAVE

Robert Webb, a farmer, was told this charming snippet of privy folklore many years ago. On the road between the villages of Bygrave and Ashwell there used to be a public house called The Knowl. At one time its only toilet was an outside bucket privy. Being built on a high and exposed site, it was very cold in winter and one bitter night the freezing conditions had turned the contents of the privy bucket into solid ice. Nevertheless, one of The Knowl's patrons was obliged to brave the cold to answer an urgent call of nature. A few minutes later he returned from the privy complaining that he had hurt his rear quarters as he sat down. 'You want to watch it when you go in there,' he said. 'Some dirty bugger's left a stander-upper!'

GOSMORE

One hears of privies being converted to all sorts of uses. Tool sheds and wood stores are probably the most common. Here at Roseview Cottage, Gosmore, near Hitchin, a Victorian red brick privy with grey slate roof was neatly transformed into a pretty hen-house for Mrs Eileen Bateman's free-range poultry. Unfortunately, shortly after the photograph was

Mrs Bateman feeding the chickens outside her Victorian privy at Gosmore.

taken, the flock was attacked by a fox and Mrs Bateman had to move the survivors somewhere safer.

GREAT MUNDEN

When Brian and Christine Cunningham took over the ancient Brockholds Farm at Great Munden in 1983, their first priority was to install lavatories and a septic tank. For the derelict farmhouse had no proper drainage and the only toilet was a three-hole privy, with a worm-eaten seat and no door, 30 yards away down the garden path.

'We had to use the privy for about 18 months,' Brian told me. 'The soil dropped down four feet into a gulley and was only flushed away when water was emptied from the kitchen sink in the house. Where it all ended up Heaven alone knows!'

Sadly, the original seat has since broken into several

Brian Cunningham with the broken seat, Great Munden.

sections but Brian has pledged to restore what may well be Hertfordshire's only surviving three-hole privy. Multi-seat loos were quite common on farms during the last century when many more workers were employed on the land. One popular design was fitted with wheels so that, when the pit beneath was full, a fresh one would be dug nearby and the privy then wheeled over it.

MANUDEN

Rhona Bird and her brother Arthur have lived in Laurel Cottage at Manuden, near Bishops Stortford, all their lives. Their privy was last used in 1962 but they still have clear memories of using it: 'Nipping out very quickly in the winter months when it was freezing but hanging things out in spring and summer, when it was tempting to sit and read the newspapers that had been torn up into squares and hung behind the door.'

The privy shed is still there, but when I visited it was filled with straw and hay for the pet rabbits. But was there anything left underneath? Arthur obliged by emptying the privy, to reveal the original box toilet, still intact after all these years.

PIRTON

'Birdie' Walker was a farm worker who I first met during the war, when we schoolboys used to help out on the local farms. Years later, in the 1960s, when our family moved to Pirton, Birdie and I met up again. By this time he was well into his eighties but still very fit and active. Every Sunday, immaculately attired, he would take a brisk stroll round the village, pausing occasionally to chat with people working in their gardens. It was during one of these chats that I asked

Arthur Bird emptying the privy at Manuden . . .

And there was the original box toilet!

Birdie how he'd kept so fit over the years.

'Liquid paraffin, boy,' he said. 'Spoonful o' liquid paraffin every mornin' soon as I get up. Clears me out nicely for the day, that does. . . . After all, the old fire won't burn bright if yer leave the ashes in the grate.'

SLEAP'S HYDE, SMALLFORD

> Presumptuous pisse-pot, how did'st thou offend?
> Compelling females on their hams to bend?
> To kings and queens we humbly bend the knee,
> But queens themselves are forced to stoop to thee.

The anonymous wit who wrote *Pisse-Pot's Farewell* in 1697 was somewhat out with his timing, because the chamber pot has remained a popular form of convenience right to the present time. Even today versions of it are used for invalids and to give toilet training to small children.

When Joy Tomkins and her family moved to Sleap's Hyde, near St Albans, in 1958 the hamlet was still in the process of 'going on the drains'. So, for a while, their only sanitary facilities were a bucket privy down the garden and a chamber pot under the bed. Now used as a wood store, Joy's old privy shed can just be seen amid the foliage. The chamber pot she is holding in the photograph has been in her family since the turn of the century and is 'still occasionally used.'

It was Joy who sent me details from a newspaper report of 1842, recording the painful death of one Mr John Clark, a retired schoolmaster. 'His death,' says the report, 'was occasioned by a piece of pot entering that part of the human frame called The Pope's Eye. On an emergency, he had occasion to resort to the use of a chamber pot which, being frail, gave way and a part pierced him and caused his death from excessive bleeding.' The report recalled grim

Joy Tomkins of Sleap's Hyde with chamber pot, and the privy just visible.

memories for Joy who still bears a three-inch scar from a similar unpleasant accident when she was a girl.

THERFIELD

A two-holer at The Grange,Therfield, has a special place in one man's memories. Gerald Drage, who lives in the village, was a farm lad at The Grange during the 1940s, when it was still a working farm. One of his daily tasks was to check the privy buckets to see if they needed emptying. If they did, he would carry them across a narrow plank bridge and spread the contents in a nearby field.

Gerald was always careful to hold the bucket handles slightly off centre so that, if the contents slopped out, they would fall away from him. 'Crossing the plank bridge to the field was quite tricky,' he said. 'Particularly on frosty mornings.'

His privy is also a wonderful example of how privy buildings can be made more attractive by planting climbing shrubs and bushes around them. Sweet-smelling honeysuckle, roses and lavender were most popular; while some owners opted for elder bushes, because they helped to keep the flies away.

A few years ago the double seat was put to good use in a rather different way. During a local fund-raising event, couples paid 50 pence a time to have their photograph taken as they sat on it together, holding hands!

[8]

LOOS FOR FAMOUS BOTTOMS

However high and mighty
With fortune, wealth or fame,
When seated on the privy
We share a common aim.

On occasions when they have had to spend a penny in some stately home, what lady hasn't sat there wondering which illustrious bottoms have preceded hers upon that wooden seat? It's certainly a thought that's caused amusement among the female members of our family from time to time! Although some owners of aristocratic piles are not always that keen to allow an investigation of their private loos, your intrepid author has been able to gain access to a few of Hertfordshire's 'country seats', where noble and even royal bottoms have rested from time to time.

The first was 18th century Brocket Hall, near Hatfield; home of the first Lord Melbourne, whose wife was mistress to King George IV. The second Lord Melbourne became Prime Minister and formed a close relationship with the young Queen Victoria, who often visited Brocket Hall and regarded him as her mentor. On Melbourne's death the Hall was inherited by his sister. She married Lord Palmerston and so it became home to a second Prime Minister of England.

There is a splendid mahogany box toilet in the bathroom of the Prime Ministers' suite at Brocket Hall. The elegant arm rests must have provided a convenient grip during more difficult moments. Since the Hall became one of Britain's leading conference centres and a venue for international summit meetings, this suite has been used by distinguished politicians from all over the world.

Brocket Hall's conference manager Kate Thomas in the bathroom of the Prince Regent's suite.

The Prime Ministers' mahogany box toilet at Brocket Hall.

The bathroom of the Prince Regent's suite also has a commode-style toilet. The carpeted block on the floor enables guests to step more easily into the high bath with its powerful old 'four-poster' shower.

Although St Paul's Walden Bury, the childhood home of Queen Elizabeth The Queen Mother, doesn't open to the public, there are occasional Open Garden Days when visitors can look round the extensive grounds. It was during one of these that I spotted a solid red-brick privy at the rear of the house. The Queen Mother's nephew, Simon Bowes Lyon, who now lives at the Bury, told me the privy was probably built in 1887 at the time of Queen Victoria's Golden Jubilee, when his grandfather, the 14th Earl of Strathmore, added a large extension to the main Queen Anne building.

The privy sits at the end of a high terrace wall. The 'chimney stack' that appears to be attached to it is no more

The privy at the rear of St Paul's Walden Bury.

than a pillar, built to provide a more decorative ending to the wall. The little room itself has probably not been used as a lavatory since Queen Elizabeth's young days in the first quarter of the century. The seat and bucket vanished long ago but the nightsoil door – through which the soil bucket would have been removed and emptied each night – is still there.

A typical Edwardian lavatory which belonged to the playwright George Bernard Shaw (1856–1950) can be seen at Shaw's Corner, the old rectory at Ayot St Lawrence where 'GBS' and his wife Charlotte lived for many years and which is now owned by the National Trust.

A commode stool brought back memories for Violet Liddle, who was employed by the Shaws as a housemaid in the 1930s. One of her duties was to wake Mrs Shaw each morning with a cup of tea and then prepare her bath. Unfortunately for Violet, Mrs Shaw refused to use either the proper bath or any of the three flush lavatories that are in the house; preferring instead to bathe in a small tub, about three feet in diameter and a foot deep, which she kept under her bed. All Mrs Shaw's other toilet needs were catered for by the commode stool which then stood in her bedroom.

Violet had no trouble recalling these household duties of 60 years ago: 'Having given Mrs Shaw her tea and under strict instructions to be as quiet as possible, I first laid out a blanket on the floor. Then, I had to get down on my hands and knees, heave out the bath from under the bed and fill it with water from two large jugs. I also had to place three towels – one soft, one medium and one rough – on the towel rail, taking care that the monograms *CFS* were facing outward. Later, when Mrs Shaw had dressed and gone downstairs, I would return to her room to empty the bath and the commode into soil buckets and make sure everything was left properly cleaned and tidy.'

75

George Bernard Shaw's lavatory at Shaw's Corner.

Charlotte Shaw's unexplained reluctance to use modern sanitaryware is all the more strange when one remembers that her husband, as a London councillor, spent years persuading the Borough of St Pancras to provide free public lavatories for women. He pointed out that it was quite unfair that men should have free urinals, while women were charged a penny – which was then quite a lot of money for poorer people to have to spend on this necessity of life. At first, Shaw's campaign appalled both residents and councillors, who protested that property values would go down. One councillor described the idea of conveniences for women as 'an abomination'. Another feared the lavatories would be misused by London's flower girls – such as for washing the violets that he occasionally bought from them for his buttonhole!

Just a few miles north of Shaw's Corner is an even more fascinating collection of historic sanitary ware which – coincidentally – also belonged to a dramatist from the Victorian era. Knebworth House, near Stevenage, was the home of the novelist and playwright Sir Edward Bulwer-Lytton, later the 1st Lord Lytton, who was a great friend of Charles Dickens. Throughout the 1850s and 1860s, Lytton's imposing mock-medieval castle was the scene of a number of literary and theatrical events in which Dickens and other leading writers and dramatists of the day took part. Nowadays, as a long-established part of Britain's stately homes industry, Knebworth is probably best known for its rock concerts. However, having been in the Lytton family for 500 years, the great house remains steeped in history and today, Bulwer-Lytton's great-great grandson, Lord Cobbold and his family have the awesome task of preserving its fabric. And it was he who kindly took me on a 'loo tour' round the private quarters of his historic house.

In a corner of the exotic Chinese bedroom, where Dickens slept during his Knebworth visits, we found the original

77

The commode Charles Dickens may have used at Knebworth.

commode that would have been at his disposal. Like the room's 18th century, hand-painted Chinese wallpaper, it is still in remarkably good condition.

In other bedrooms are elegant examples of a commode and a chamber pot cupboard fashioned in the popular Franco-Italian designs of the late 18th and early 19th centuries. This furniture was brought to the house by Elizabeth Bulwer-Lytton in 1812 when she restored the building to its present gothic style, after it had been empty for 50 years. In the photograph of the open commode note, on the floor, the beautifully turned wooden lid that fits over the pot, hopefully to seal in offensive smells!

These days, there is little left of Knebworth's original Victorian plumbing. 'Sadly, my father had this thing about taking out all the old-fashioned pieces and replacing them with modern ceramics,' Lord Cobbold told me somewhat wistfully. Consequently, the only piece of fixed ceramic ware of any historic importance is an art-deco wash basin which visitors to the ladies' public toilet are still able to use. It is the only surviving example of the ceramic ware designed for Knebworth House by Sir Edwin Lutyens – a brother-in-law of the Lytton family – in the early 1900s. However, something has now been done to redress the situation.

'Each generation has contributed to the character and history of the house,' Lord Cobbold writes in his brochure to Knebworth. One of his own contributions has been to commission a stained glass window to commemorate the 25th anniversary of the Knebworth rock concerts. The window conceals another surprise. Behind it is a superb re-creation of a 'Victorian Gentlemen's Toilet', filled with a marvellous collection of memorabilia of the Lytton-Cobbold family that is sure to keep guests detained in His Lordship's smallest room twice as long as they need be!

A French-style commode, open to show the interior.

A chamber pot cupboard, handily placed.

Lord Cobbold and the stained glass window he commissioned.

Inside the Victorian Gentlemen's Toilet, filled with memorabilia.

[9]

A Privy Pot-Pourri

It's no use standing on the seat
The crabs in here can jump six feet.
(From the cubicle door of a gents' toilet in Stevenage)

While most of the graffiti in public lavatories doesn't bear repetition, privy poets and artists occasionally come up with a gem. One that tickled Dr Robert Parsons of Hemel Hempstead was a sign pointing to the six-inch gap between the bottom of the door and the floor, reading: 'Beware of Limbo Dancers!'

Back in the 1940s, the village school at Codicote had a talented graffiti artist – the headmaster! According to Iris Newbold of Knebworth, who taught there, Mr Ewart Wesley would go into the staff toilet armed with a pencil and pass the time making comical faces and figures out of the knots in the wooden partitioning. 'He was a good cartoonist,' Mrs Newbold said. 'Some of the drawings were very funny and took your mind off the bleak conditions of that time. We used to laugh at the fact that, while we would always tell the children off if we caught them writing on a wall, their headmaster was happily scribbling away on the one in the staff toilet!'

━━━━━━━━━━

Mrs Rose Rose, of Letchworth, related a true story told to her by a neighbour when they lived in a row of cottages in Mill Road, Royston. During the 1920s, each cottage had a privy at

Mrs Rose's cartoon of the unexpected occupant of her neighbour's privy at Royston.

the bottom of the garden. Late one evening the neighbour's mother-in-law, a Mrs Rayment, set off down the garden path to make herself comfortable for the night. On opening the privy door she discovered it was occupied by a bear!

Having recovered from the initial shock, Mrs Rayment then realised that the bear's owner was also in there, sitting on the toilet. The embarrassed man explained that he was a street entertainer who was staying at a lodging house in the next street. Not impressed by the toilets there, he had spotted Mrs Rayment's tidy privy and decided to use that instead. He dare not leave the bear with anyone else in case it was stolen or escaped. So it always went everywhere with him – even to the toilet!

Terry di Francesco and his restaurant in St Albans converted from a former public toilet.

For most of the century the little Edwardian building in Hatfield Road, St Albans, served the purpose for which it was built – as a Ladies' and Gentlemen's convenience for people enjoying the facilities of Clarence Park. In 1977, after a serious assault had occurred in the lavatories, the city council decided to close the building and it remained boarded up for the next 14 years.

Then, in 1991, it was spotted by an Italian-born resident Mr Terry Di Francesco, who had the bright idea of turning it into a restaurant. Terry approached the council with his plan, offering to restore and convert the building at his own expense. He now has it on a 30-year lease and 'Verdi's Trattoria' is one of two former public toilets in St Albans which the enterprising Terry has transformed into popular eating houses for the community.

The goldfish, quite happy in the cistern.

At first glance, maintenance worker Chris Armstead over the page appears in the photograph to be servicing the cistern for the gents' urinal down in the ancient basement of Brocket Hall. In fact, he is feeding the occupants. For as long as anyone can remember the glass-sided Victorian cistern has been home for a small school of goldfish and it's one of Chris's jobs to feed them each day. Visitors have occasionally expressed concern for the fishes' welfare but, in fact, they are very happy. Unlike the occupants of many aquariums, these get a steady supply of fresh water every time the cistern flushes. The mechanism is adjusted to ensure that there is always sufficient water left in the bottom.

Behind the door of an ivy-clad loo in the village of Hertingfordbury is a sample of the work of the most celebrated name in England's lavatorial history . . . a 100

Feeding the fish at Brocket Hall!

Jeremy Secker's ivy-clad privy at Hertingfordbury.

The most celebrated name in lavatorial history!

year old flushing cistern bearing the name of Crapper. Although 'The Leverett' was not one of Mr Crapper's most exotic models, it is still much valued by its owner, Jeremy Secker, who purchased it from another resident in the village after his outside loo had been accidentally damaged by a workman's digger.

Thomas Crapper (1837–1910) was a talented sanitary engineer who patented a number of improved toilet systems and made his reputation when he won a contract to provide new loos at Royal Sandringham. In America today, Crapper's name is to toilets what Hoover's is to vacuum cleaners. It was taken back to the United States by US servicemen stationed in England during the First World War. Many were lads from remote farming regions who had only ever known bucket privies and were fascinated by the gleaming white bowls bearing Thomas Crapper's insignia. By 1930, according to *The Dictionary of American Slang*, 'going to the crapper' was a phrase used by many Americans.

The word *crap* itself had been around a long time before Mr Crapper. Over the centuries it has been used to describe chaff and the refuse left over from fat boiling. In Thomas Crapper's biography *Flushed with Pride*, Wallace Reyburn mentions an 1891 book on Victorian slang words in which *crap* is given a variety of meanings including 'to harvest' and 'to ease oneself'. Nowadays, *The Concise Oxford Dictionary* lists it firstly as meaning 'nonsense' (as in 'he talks crap') and secondly as 'faeces' – adding that it is still usually considered a taboo word. All of which leads us neatly to the *Hertfordshire Privies* glossary of words that have been adopted (or invented) to describe our toilets and what we do in them.

A PRIVY BY ANY OTHER NAME

I first heard my favourite lavatory euphemism from the wife of a good friend, when I called one morning to check on his condition after our evening out. 'Well, he's spent most of the night talking to God on the great white telephone,' she said. Thus providing an instant picture of her husband with his head in the lavatory bowl, moaning 'Oh God!' as he threw up for the upteenth time.

While every family has its favourite word for the lavatory and the process of relieving oneself, there are some expressions that defy the word *euphemism* because they sound worse than the act itself. So here, from the delicate to the downright coarse, are some of the phrases heard when men and women announce their departure from the room to visit the toilet:

'Excuse me. I'm just going out to. . . .
Browse in the reading room
Call on Winnie (Winston Churchill – WC)
Check my tackle
Check the decorations
Do a dump
Do a gruntie
Do job-jobs
Do a nicky-noo
Do a poo (or pookie)
Do a tinkle
Do a tomtit
Do a trickle
Have a shit
Have a slash
Inspect the plumbing
Pay a visit
Pick a daisy
Pluck a rose
Point Percy at the porcelain
Ride the porcelain pony
See a man about a dog
See a friend off to the coast
See if the tap's running
See which way the wind's blowing
Shed a tear for Lord Nelson
Spend a penny
Splash my boots
Stack my tools
Strain the potatoes (or greens)
Try for the Big One
Try the Throne for size
Visit the heads
Visit Tinkerbell
Water the flowers.

For the privy itself, here are more than a hundred
affectionate nicknames – to which the reader can probably
add a few more.

A certain place
Astor Room
Aunt Jane's
Back house
Biffy
Bog
Boghouse
Bombay
Chamber of Commerce
Chamberlain Pianos
    ('bucket lav')
Chuggie
Clodgie
Closet
Comfort station
Crap box
Crap castle
Crap house
Crapper
Crapping kennel
Dike
Dinkum-dunnies
Dispensary
Doneks
Dover Castle
Dubby
Dubs
Duffs
Dunnakin
Dunnekin

Dunnick
Dunnickin
Dunny
Dyke
Garden loo
Garderobe
George
Glory hole
Gong house
Great white telephone
Grot
Halting Station Hoojyboo
    (att. to Dame Edith
    Evans)
Heads
Holy of holies
Home of rest
Honk
House of Commons
House of Relief
Hummer
Jakes
Jam pot
Japping
Jericho
Jerry-cum-tumble
John
Karzi
Klondike
Knickies

Larties
Latrine
Lats
Lav
Lavatory
Little boys' room
Little girls' room
Little house
Long drop
Loo
My aunts
Necessary
Nessy
Netty
Opportunity
Out the back
Petty
Ping pong house
Place of easement
Place of repose
Place of retirement
Powder room
Proverbial
Reading room
Reredorter
Round the back
Sammy

Sentry box
Shants
Shit hole
Shittus (shit house)
Shooting gallery
Shot tower
Shunkie
Slash house
Smallest room
Tandem (a two-holer)
Thinking room
Throne room
Thunder box
Tivvy
Toilet
Umtag (from the Russian
  for WC)
Urals
Urinal
Watering hole
Waterloo
Watteries
Wee house
What-yer-callit
Widdlehouse
Windsor Castle
'Yer Tiz'